Perfect Food for After School

After-school food solutions from snack attacks to super suppers

This edition published in 2010
LOVE FOOD is an imprint of Parragon Books Ltd

Parragon
Queen Street House
4 Queen Street
Bath BA1 1HE, UK

ISBN: 978-1-4454-1634-2

Printed in China

Photography: Mike Cooper
Introduction text: Beverly Le Blanc
Food stylist: Sumi Glass (cover) and Lincoln Jefferson (recipes)
Cover and internal design: Sarah Knight
Cover models: Carly Lou, Harry and Tilly Glass

Notes for the Reader
This book uses imperial, metric, and US cup measurements. Follow the same units of measurement throughout; do not mix imperial and metric. All spoon measurements are level: teaspoons are assumed to be 5 ml, and tablespoons are assumed to be 15 ml. Unless otherwise stated, milk is assumed to be whole, eggs and individual vegetables are medium, and pepper is freshly ground black pepper.

The times given are an approximate guide only. Preparation times differ according to the techniques used by different people and the cooking times may also vary from those given. Optional ingredients, variations, or serving suggestions have not been included in the calculations.

Recipes using raw or very lightly cooked eggs should be avoided by infants, the elderly, pregnant women, convalescents, and anyone with a chronic condition. Pregnant and breast-feeding women are advised to avoid eating peanuts and peanut products. People with a nut allergy should be aware that some of the prepared ingredients used in the recipes in this book may contain nuts. Always check the packaging before use.

Contents

Introduction

As every parent or carer knows, it is a challenge to get young school children to eat healthily. But it is a challenge worth accepting, because if they develop good eating habits at an early age, they will reap the benefits throughout their adult lives. The greater variety of foods your children eat every day, the more likely they are to get all the essential vitamins and minerals they need for their growing and developing bodies. And what your children eat when they come home hungry from school can have long-lasting effects. Try substituting Chicken and Apple Bites (see page 14) for a package of potato chips, and get your children into the habit of eating healthy snacks.

EATING WELL FOR LIFE
High-profile campaigns have highlighted the important role a healthy diet plays in everything from children's overall health and behavior to their concentration and performance in the classroom. Ideally, their diet—like your diet—should include plenty of fruit and vegetables, cereals, rice, pasta, bread and potatoes, with small amounts of lean meat, poultry, fish, eggs, and legumes.

Foods high in fat, sugar, and salt should only be eaten occasionally. As youngsters leisure time activities move from the playground to the computer, obesity is increasing at an alarming rate. Ways to counter this trend include offering water or milk instead of sweetened soda pops, and fruit and vegetables rather than sugary cookies and cakes—save those for occasional treats, rather than everyday snacks.

Actually getting kids to eat food that is good for them

is easier said than done. Most children will choose a package of potato chips over a healthier option every day of the week, and school-age children are notoriously fussy eaters. Perfect Food for After School, however, can help you achieve your goal with yummy, healthy recipes that make snacks and mealtimes pleasurable.

STRONG BONES!
School-age children need a variety of vitamins and minerals every day for optimum health, and calcium is a particularly important nutrient, as it is essential for healthy bones and teeth. Whole milk, yogurt, and small amounts of cheese are all excellent sources. Or try desserts such as Chocolate Mousse (see page 43) and Mini Strawberry Cheesecakes (see page 46)—they will be hard to resist!

GO FOR 5
We are all encouraged to eat five portions of fruit and vegetables every day, because they are such a good source of vitamins, minerals, and fiber. But as most parents know, getting children to eat one portion, let alone five, is not easy. You'll find imaginative ideas for incorporating vegetables into tasty main courses in 'The Vegetable Garden' chapter, beginning on page 28. And don't forget tempting yet healthy desserts, such as Fruit Skewers (see page 40).

SETTING AN EXAMPLE
Always remember young children learn by copying adults, so the best way to encourage healthy eating is for you to choose the healthy options and set regular mealtimes. Mix and match recipes in the 'Making a Meal of It' and 'The Vegetable Garden' chapters, and the whole family will benefit.

Snack Stop

Regular meals and healthy snacks should provide a framework for a good diet with the right balance of nutrients and calorie content.

Good nutrition will not only benefit your child's health, but may also improve his or her behavior, and general well-being.

Broiled Cheese Sandwich

★ Preheat the broiler. Slice the crusty top off the loaf; reserve for another use. Slice the loaf into two layers, making the bottom layer thicker. Place the bottom layer on a large piece of aluminum foil.

★ Toast the top surface of the top layer of the loaf until brown, then turn it and place on the foil.

★ Sprinkle a heaping ¾ cup of cheese over both layers of bread. Arrange the avocado and tomato wedges on the bottom layer, then sprinkle with half the remaining cheese. Top with the asparagus spears and ham, completely covering the edges of the ingredients underneath. Sprinkle with the remaining cheese and a drizzle of olive oil.

★ Cook well away from the heat source for 3–5 minutes. Remove the plain cheese-topped layer first, when the cheese is bubbling. Cook the bottom layer until the cheese has melted and the ham is browned.

★ Cut the filled layer into four pieces. Cut the toasted cheese layer into 8 wedges and overlap 2 wedges on each of the four pieces. Serve at once.

1 stone-ground buckwheat boule loaf (about 7 inch/ 17.5 cm diameter) or other rustic round loaf

1½ cups finely shaved or coarsely grated cheddar cheese

1 large avocado, halved, pitted, peeled, and sliced

2 tomatoes, halved and cut into fine wedges

12 canned asparagus spears, cooked

4 slices Parma, Serrano, or Black Forest ham

olive oil, for drizzling

SERVES 4

Bean & Pasta Soup

★ Heat the olive oil in a large, heavy-bottom saucepan. Add the onion, celery, and carrot and cook over medium heat for 8–10 minutes, stirring occasionally, until the vegetables have softened.

★ Add the bay leaf, stock, and chopped tomatoes, then bring to a boil. Reduce the heat, cover, and simmer for 15 minutes, or until the vegetables are just tender.

★ Add the pasta and beans, then bring the soup back to a boil and cook for 10 minutes, or until the pasta is just tender. Stir occasionally to prevent the pasta from sticking to the bottom of the pan and burning.

★ Season to taste with salt and pepper. Remove and discard the bay leaf. Add the spinach, and cook for another two minutes, or until tender. Serve immediately, sprinkled with Parmesan cheese.

4 tbsp olive oil

1 onion, finely chopped

1 celery stalk, chopped

1 carrot, peeled and diced

1 bay leaf

5 cups low-sodium or homemade vegetable stock

14 oz/400 g canned chopped tomatoes

6 oz/175 g pasta shapes, such as farfalle, shells, or twists

14 oz/400 g canned cannellini beans, drained and rinsed

7 oz/200 g spinach or Swiss chard, thick stalks removed and shredded

salt and pepper

⅓ cup Parmesan cheese finely grated, to serve

SERVES 4

Creamy Tomato Soup

★ Melt the butter in a large pan over low heat and cook the onion, leek, and garlic for 10 minutes, or until very soft but not browned.

★ Add the carrot and potato and cook for 5 minutes.

★ Add the stock and bring to simmering point.

★ Add the tomatoes and tomato paste and season to taste with salt and pepper. Let simmer for 15 minutes, until the vegetables are very soft. Add the milk and warm through, then transfer the soup to a blender or food processor and process until very smooth. You can pass the soup through a strainer at this stage, if you like.

★ Return the soup to the rinsed-out pan and reheat gently. Garnish the soup with snipped chives, if desired, and serve immediately with whole wheat rolls.

1 tbsp butter

½ red onion, minced

1 leek, chopped

1 garlic clove, crushed

1 carrot, peeled and grated

1 potato, peeled and grated

1½ cups low-sodium or homemade vegetable stock

1 lb 2 oz/500 g ripe tomatoes, peeled, seeded, and chopped

1 tbsp tomato paste

⅔ cup whole milk

salt and pepper

snipped chives, to garnish (optional)

whole wheat rolls, to serve

SERVES 4

Pizza Fingers

★ To make the pizza dough, place the flour, salt, and yeast in a bowl. Make a well in the center of the flour and add the water and oil, then mix with a knife until the mixture forms a soft dough.

★ Turn out onto a lightly floured work surface and knead for 5 minutes. Cover and let rest for 5 minutes. Knead again for an additional 5 minutes until the dough is elastic. Place in a lightly oiled bowl and cover with plastic wrap. Let stand in a warm place for 45 minutes, or until doubled in size. Preheat the oven to 425°F/220°C.

★ Knead the risen dough lightly, and then roll out to form a rough rectangle and place in an oiled rectangular baking pan. If you are not using a baking pan, place the base on a lightly oiled cookie sheet and push up the edges of the dough to form a shallow rim.

★ Spoon the tomato pizza sauce over the dough. Top one quarter of the dough with the cooked spinach, a second quarter with tuna, a third quarter with the yellow bell pepper and the remaining quarter with salami. Break up the mozzarella cheese with your fingers and sprinkle it over the toppings. Sprinkle over the cheddar cheese. Season with salt and pepper to taste and drizzle with a little warmed olive oil.

★ Bake in the top of the preheated oven for 12–15 minutes, until the topping is slightly crisp and golden. Slice into strips and serve immediately.

PIZZA DOUGH

1 ⅔ cup white bread flour, sifted, plus extra for dusting

1 tsp salt

½ tsp easy-blend yeast

⅔ cup warm water

1 tbsp olive oil, plus extra for greasing

6 oz/175 g canned low-sodium tomato pizza sauce

TOPPINGS

handful of cooked fresh spinach leaves, tough stalks removed, shredded, and squeezed dry

2¾ oz/75 g canned tuna in oil, drained

½ yellow or orange bell pepper, seeded and finely sliced

4 slices salami

4 oz/115 g mozzarella cheese

¾ cup shredded cheddar cheese

salt and pepper

olive oil, for drizzling

SERVES 2

Chicken & Apple Bites

★ Spread the apple out on a clean dish towel and press out all the excess moisture.

★ Put the apple, chicken, onion, parsley, breadcrumbs, and stock in a food processor or blender and blend briefly until well combined.

★ Spread the flour out on a plate. Divide the mixture into 20 mini portions, shape each portion into a ball, and roll in the flour.

★ Heat a little oil in a nonstick skillet over medium heat and cook the balls for 5–8 minutes, or until golden brown all over and cooked through. Remove and drain on paper towels. Serve hot, or cold for a lunchbox.

1 apple, peeled, cored, and grated

2 skinless, boneless chicken breasts, cut into chunks

½ red onion, minced

1 tbsp minced fresh parsley

scant 1 cup fresh whole wheat breadcrumbs

1 tbsp concentrated chicken stock

whole wheat flour, for coating

peanut oil, for pan-frying

MAKES 20

Making a Meal of It

Don't overload your child's plate. It is very off-putting for children to be presented with huge piles of food with you expecting them to eat it all. Instead, give them manageable portions—it's always better that they ask for a little more than reject a whole plate.

17

Tuna Noodle Casserole

★ Preheat the oven to 400°F/200°C. Bring a large pan of salted water to a boil. Add the pasta, then return to a boil and cook for 2 minutes less than specified on the package directions.

★ Meanwhile, melt the butter in a separate small pan. Stir in the breadcrumbs, then remove from the heat and set aside.

★ Drain the pasta well and set aside. Pour the soup into the pasta pan over medium heat, then stir in the milk, celery, bell peppers, half the cheese, and all the parsley. Add the tuna and gently stir in so that the flakes don't break up. Season to taste with salt and pepper. Heat just until small bubbles appear around the edge of the mixture—do not boil.

★ Stir the pasta into the pan and use 2 forks to mix all the ingredients together. Spoon the mixture into an ovenproof dish that is also suitable for serving, and spread it out.

★ Stir the remaining cheese into the buttered breadcrumbs, then sprinkle over the top of the pasta mixture. Bake in the preheated oven for 20–25 minutes, or until the topping is golden. Remove from the oven, then let stand for 5 minutes before serving.

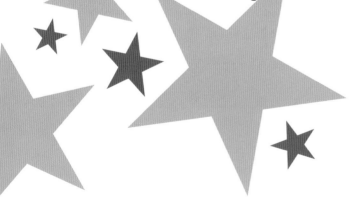

7 oz/200 g dried ribbon egg pasta, such as tagliatelle

2 tbsp butter

1 cup fine fresh breadcrumbs

1⅔ cups canned condensed cream of mushroom soup

½ cup milk

2 celery stalks, chopped

1 red bell pepper, seeded and chopped

1 green bell pepper, seeded and chopped

1¼ cups coarsely grated sharp cheddar cheese

2 tbsp chopped fresh parsley

7 oz/200 g canned tuna in oil, drained and flaked

salt and pepper

SERVES 4–6

Fish Sticks & Potato Wedges

★ Preheat the oven to 400°F/200°C.

★ To make the potato wedges, dry the sweet potatoes on a clean dish towel. Place the oil in a roasting pan and heat for a few minutes in the oven. Arrange the potatoes in the pan and bake for 30–35 minutes, turning them halfway through, until tender and golden.

★ Meanwhile, cut the cod into strips about ³⁄₄-inch/2-cm wide.

★ Put the flour onto a plate, add the paprika, and season to taste with salt and pepper. Put the breadcrumbs onto a second plate. Roll the cod strips in the seasoned flour until coated, shaking off any excess, then dip them in the beaten egg. Roll the cod strips in the breadcrumbs until evenly coated.

★ Heat enough oil to cover the bottom of a large, nonstick skillet. Carefully arrange the fish sticks in the pan—you may have to cook them in batches—and fry them for 3–4 minutes on each side, or until crisp and golden. Drain on paper towels before serving, if necessary.

★ Serve the fish sticks immediately with the sweet potato wedges and peas.

10 oz/280 g thick cod fillets, skin and bones removed

flour, for dusting

1 tsp paprika

fresh breadcrumbs or fine cornmeal, for coating

1 egg, beaten

sunflower oil, for frying

salt and pepper

freshly cooked peas, to serve

SWEET POTATO WEDGES

2 large sweet potatoes, scrubbed and cut into wedges

1 tbsp olive oil

MAKES 8–10 FISH STICKS

Salmon Cakes

★ Preheat the oven to 400°F/200°C. Put the salmon in a pan with the milk and bay leaf and bring slowly to simmering point. Let simmer for 2 minutes, then remove the pan from the heat, lift out and discard the bay leaf, and let the fish stand in the milk to cool. When cool, lift out the fish with a slotted spoon onto paper towels to drain.

★ Flake the fish into a large bowl. Put the broccoli in a food processor and blend until smooth. Add to the fish with the mashed potatoes, parsley, 1 tablespoon of the flour, and pepper to taste. Add the egg yolk and mix well. If the mixture is a little dry, add some of the poaching milk; if too wet, add a little more flour.

★ Divide the mixture into 12 portions and shape each portion into a cake. Put the beaten eggs, remaining flour, and the breadcrumbs on 3 separate plates. Roll each fish cake in the flour, then in the beaten egg, and then in the breadcrumbs to coat.

★ Heat the oil in a nonstick baking sheet in the preheated oven for 5 minutes. Add the fish cakes and bake for 10 minutes, then carefully turn them over and bake for an additional 10 minutes. Serve immediately.

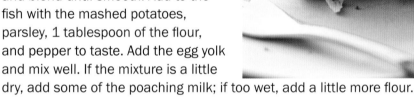

1 lb 9 oz/700 g skinless salmon fillet, cut into cubes

1¼ cups whole milk

1 bay leaf

1½ cups broccoli florets

1 lb 9 oz/700 g potatoes, boiled and mashed

2 tbsp minced fresh parsley

4 tbsp whole wheat all-purpose flour

1 egg yolk

2 large eggs, beaten

2¾ cups fresh whole wheat breadcrumbs

2 tbsp olive oil

pepper

MAKES 12

Bacon, Pea & Potato Frittata

★ Preheat the broiler to high. Cook the bacon under the broiler until crisp. Let cool slightly, then cut into small pieces and set aside.

★ Heat the oil in a large, heavy-bottom skillet with a heatproof handle and cook the onion, stirring occasionally, for 8 minutes, or until softened.

★ Add the potatoes and cook, turning frequently to prevent them from sticking to the skillet, for 5 minutes, or until golden. Add the bacon and baby peas, then spread the mixture evenly over the bottom of the skillet.

★ Reheat the broiler to high. Season the beaten eggs with salt and pepper, then pour carefully over the onion-and-potato mixture. Cook over medium heat for 5–6 minutes, or until the eggs are just set and the bottom of the frittata is lightly golden brown.

★ Place the skillet under the broiler and cook the top for 3 minutes, or until set and lightly golden. Serve the frittata warm or cold, cut into wedges or slices, with fresh tomato wedges.

2–3 slices good-quality bacon

1½ tbsp olive oil

1 onion, very finely chopped

12 oz/350 g new potatoes, cooked, and halved or quartered, if large

½ cup frozen baby peas

6 eggs, lightly beaten

salt and pepper

tomato wedges, to serve

SERVES 3–4

Spaghetti with Meat Sauce

★ To make the sauce, heat the oil in a heavy-bottom skillet. Add the onion and sauté, half covered, for 5 minutes, or until softened. Add the garlic, carrot, and mushrooms, if using, and sauté for another 3 minutes, stirring occasionally.

★ Add the herbs and ground beef to the pan and cook until the meat has browned, stirring regularly.

★ Add the stock and strained tomatoes. Reduce the heat, season to taste, and cook over a medium–low heat, half covered, for 15–20 minutes, or until the sauce has reduced and thickened. Remove and discard the bay leaf.

★ Meanwhile, bring a large pan of salted water to the boil. Add the pasta, then return to a boil and cook for 8–10 minutes, or according to the package directions, until tender but firm to the bite. Drain well and mix together the pasta and sauce until the pasta is well coated. Serve immediately, sprinkled with the grated Parmesan cheese, if liked.

12 oz/350 g spaghetti or pasta of your choice

grated Parmesan cheese, for sprinkling (optional)

MEAT SAUCE

2 tbsp olive oil

1 onion, finely chopped

2 garlic cloves, finely chopped

1 carrot, peeled and finely chopped

1½ cups mushrooms, peeled and sliced or chopped (optional)

1 tsp dried oregano

½ tsp dried thyme

1 bay leaf

10 oz/280 g lean ground beef

1¼ cups stock

1¼ cups strained tomatoes

pepper

SERVES 4

Homemade Chicken Nuggets

★ Preheat the oven to 375°F/190°C. Cut the chicken breasts into 1½-inch/4-cm chunks. Mix the flour, wheat germ, cumin, coriander, and pepper to taste in a bowl, then divide in half and put on 2 separate plates. Put the beaten egg on a third plate.

★ Pour the oil into a baking sheet and heat in the preheated oven. Roll the chicken pieces in one plate of flour, shake to remove any excess, then roll in the egg and in the second plate of flour, again shaking off any excess flour. When all the nuggets are ready, remove the baking sheet from the oven and toss the nuggets in the hot oil. Roast in the oven for 25–30 minutes, until golden and crisp.

★ Meanwhile, to make the dipping sauce, put both kinds of tomatoes in a blender or food processor and process until smooth. Add the mayonnaise and process again until well combined.

★ Remove the nuggets from the oven and drain on paper towels. Serve immediately with the dipping sauce.

3 skinless, boneless chicken breasts

4 tbsp whole wheat all-purpose flour

1 tbsp wheat germ

½ tsp ground cumin

½ tsp ground coriander

pepper

1 egg, lightly beaten

2 tbsp olive oil

DIPPING SAUCE

1 cup drained, sun-dried tomatoes

½ cup peeled, seeded, and chopped fresh tomatoes

2 tbsp mayonnaise

SERVES 4

The Vegetable Garden

Make sure that you vary the fruit and vegetables in your child's diet, mixing up the colors.

In fact, get your children to chose which fruit and vegetables they will have when shopping, but don't worry if they refuse some items, as long as they have a good mix.

Creamy Pasta Casserole

★ Preheat the oven to 375°F/190°C. Bring a large pan of salted water to the boil. Add the pasta, then return to a boil and cook for 8–10 minutes, or according to the package directions, until tender but firm to the bite. Drain well.

★ Meanwhile, heat the oil in a large skillet and cook the mushrooms until beginning to brown. Boil or steam the broccoli until just cooked, then drain.

★ Add the chicken to the mushrooms and stir well. Blend the cornstarch with a little milk in a pitcher, then gradually add the remaining milk, stirring. Pour into the skillet with the mushrooms, add the sour cream, and warm through, stirring.

★ Add the pasta and broccoli to the skillet and season to taste with salt and pepper. Mix well, then transfer to a baking dish, top with the cheese, and bake in the preheated oven for 15 minutes. Serve immediately.

6 oz/175 g whole wheat pasta shells

1 tbsp olive oil

1¾ cups quartered button mushrooms

1 broccoli crown, broken into small florets

2 cooked skinless, boneless chicken breasts, shredded

1 tbsp cornstarch

scant 1 cup milk

½ cup light sour cream

½ cup shredded cheddar cheese

salt and pepper

SERVES 4

Roasted Vegetable Lasagne

★ Preheat the oven to 375°F/190°C. Put the oil in a large bowl, add the zucchini, bell peppers, eggplant, onions, and shallots and toss well to coat.

★ Divide the vegetables between 2 baking sheets and roast in the preheated oven for 30–40 minutes, until soft and flecked with brown. Add the button mushrooms after 20 minutes.

★ Remove the vegetables from the oven and put into a large bowl. Add the tomatoes and tomato paste and mix well.

★ Melt the butter in a pan over low heat. Stir in the flour and cook, stirring constantly, for 2–3 minutes. Gradually add the milk and cook, continuing to stir constantly, until the sauce is thick and smooth. Season to taste with salt and pepper and stir in the cheddar cheese.

★ Layer the vegetable mixture and sauce in an ovenproof dish with the lasagna noodles, finishing with a layer of sauce. Sprinkle over the Parmesan cheese and bake in the oven for 30–35 minutes.

★ Remove from the oven and serve immediately with a green salad.

3 tbsp olive oil

4 zucchini, halved lengthwise and thickly sliced

3 red bell peppers, seeded and chopped

1 eggplant, chopped

2 red onions, chopped

5 shallots, peeled and quartered

9 oz/250 g button mushrooms

14 oz/400 g canned chopped tomatoes

1 tbsp tomato paste

3½ tbsp butter

heaping ⅓ cup all-purpose flour or gluten-free flour

2½ cups milk

heaping ⅓ cup grated cheddar cheese

7 oz/200 g fresh lasagna noodles

2 tbsp grated Parmesan cheese

salt and pepper

green salad, to serve

SERVES 4

Garlic Potato Wedges

★ Bring a large pan of water to the boil, add the potatoes, and parboil them for 10 minutes. Drain the potatoes, refresh under cold water, and then drain them again thoroughly.

★ Transfer the potatoes to a cutting board. When the potatoes are cold enough to handle, cut them into thick wedges, but do not peel.

★ Preheat the broiler. Heat the oil and butter in a small pan together with the garlic. Cook gently until the garlic begins to brown, then remove the pan from the heat.

★ Stir the herbs and seasoning into the mixture in the pan.

★ Brush the herb-and-butter mixture all over the potato wedges.

★ Cook under the broiler for 10–15 minutes, or until the potato wedges are just tender, brushing liberally with any of the remaining herb-and-butter mixture.

★ Transfer the garlic potato wedges to a warmed serving plate and serve immediately.

3 large baking potatoes, scrubbed

4 tbsp olive oil

2 tbsp butter

2 garlic cloves, chopped

1 tbsp chopped fresh rosemary

1 tbsp chopped fresh parsley

1 tbsp chopped fresh thyme

salt and pepper

SERVES 4

Bean Burgers

★ Mash the beans with a potato masher in a bowl until they are smooth, then add the pesto, breadcrumbs, egg, season to taste with salt and pepper, and mix well.

★ Heat half the oil in a skillet over low heat and cook the onion and garlic until softened. Add to the bean mixture and mix well.

★ Heat the remaining oil in the skillet. Spoon in the bean mixture, in 6 separate mounds, then press each one down with the back of a spoon to form a burger.

★ Cook the burgers for 4–5 minutes, then carefully turn over and cook for an additional 4–5 minutes, until golden.

★ Meanwhile, slice the rolls in half and smear each one with hummus.

★ Remove the burgers from the skillet and drain on paper towels. Place each one in a roll, top with the tomatoes, cucumber, and salad greens, and serve immediately.

14 oz/400 g canned cannellini beans, drained and rinsed

2 tbsp red pesto

scant 1½ cups fresh whole wheat breadcrumbs

1 egg

2 tbsp olive oil

½ small red onion, minced

1 garlic clove, crushed

6 whole wheat rolls

6 tsp hummus

salt and pepper

6 cherry tomatoes, sliced

sliced cucumber or pickles

salad greens, to serve

MAKES 6

Chinese Noodles

★ Mix together the ingredients for the marinade in a shallow dish. Add the tofu and spoon the marinade over. Refrigerate for 1 hour to marinate, turning the tofu occasionally to let the flavors steep.

★ Preheat the oven to 400°F/200°C. Using a slotted spoon, remove the tofu from the marinade and reserve the liquid. Arrange the tofu on a baking sheet and roast for 20 minutes, turning occasionally, until the tofu pieces are golden and crisp on all sides.

★ Meanwhile, cook the noodles according to the package directions, then drain. Rinse the noodles under cold running water and drain again.

★ Heat a wok or heavy-bottom skillet, then add the oil. Add the bell pepper, broccoli, and corn and stir-fry, tossing and stirring continuously, over a medium–high heat for 5–8 minutes, or until the vegetables have softened. Add the water and continue to stir-fry until the vegetables are just tender but remain slightly crunchy.

★ Stir in the marinade, noodles, tofu, and scallions and stir-fry until heated through. Serve immediately sprinkled with sesame seeds, if using.

9 oz/250 g tofu, drained and cubed

9 oz/250 g medium egg noodles

1 tbsp peanut or vegetable oil

1 red bell pepper, deseeded and sliced

3 cups broccoli florets

12 baby corn, halved lengthwise

2–3 tbsp water

2 scallions, finely sliced

1 tbsp sesame seeds, toasted, to serve (optional)

MARINADE

1 garlic clove, finely chopped

1-inch/2.5-cm piece fresh ginger, peeled and grated

1 tsp sesame oil

1 tbsp honey

2 tbsp dark soy sauce

SERVES 4

Sweet Treats!

It is virtually impossible to insulate your children against the might of the fast-food giants, but if they really do want a sweet treat, then ensure their treats are homemade—making them instantly healthier and giving you peace of mind that you know exactly every ingredient used.

Fruit Skewers

★ Soak 4 bamboo skewers in water for at least 20 minutes.

★ Preheat the broiler to high and line the broiler pan with foil. Thread alternate pieces of fruit onto each skewer. Brush the fruit with a little maple syrup.

★ Put the chocolate in a heatproof bowl, set the bowl over a pan of barely simmering water, and heat until it is melted.

★ Meanwhile, cook the fruit skewers under the preheated broiler for 3 minutes, or until caramelized. Serve immediately drizzled with a little of the melted chocolate, removing the fruit from the skewer if serving to younger children.

selection of fruit, such as apricots, peaches, figs, strawberries, mangoes, pineapple, bananas, dates, and papaya, prepared and cut into chunks

maple syrup

1¾ oz/50 g semisweet dark chocolate (minimum 70% cocoa solids), broken into chunks

MAKES 4

Ice Cream Strawberry Sundae

★ To make the sauce, put the strawberries in a blender with the orange juice and process until smooth. Transfer the mixture to a saucepan and add the sugar. Cook over a medium heat for 10–12 minutes, or until thickened. Let cool.

★ To serve, place a spoonful of the strawberry sauce in the bottom of a tall glass. Add two scoops of ice cream and another spoonful of fruit sauce. Sprinkle with the nuts and chocolate. Arrange the marshmallows on top. Repeat to make four sundaes and serve immediately.

8 scoops of good-quality vanilla ice cream

¼ cup chopped mixed nuts, lightly toasted in a dry skillet

grated chocolate and marshmallows, to serve

STRAWBERRY SAUCE

1½ cups hulled and halved strawberries

2 tbsp freshly squeezed orange juice

2 tbsp superfine sugar

SERVES 4

Chocolate Mousse

★ Put the chocolate and butter in a heatproof bowl, set the bowl over a saucepan of barely simmering water and heat until melted. Let cool slightly, then stir in the egg yolks, maple syrup, and yogurt.

★ Whisk the egg whites in a large, grease-free bowl until stiff, then fold into the chocolate mixture. Divide between 6 small ramekins and chill for 4 hours.

★ Meanwhile, put the blueberries in a small saucepan with the water and cook until the berries begin to pop and turn glossy. Let cool, then chill.

★ Serve immediately, topped with a few blueberries and a little grated white chocolate.

3½ oz/100 g semisweet dark chocolate (minimum 70% cocoa solids), chopped

1 tbsp butter

2 large eggs, separated

1 tbsp maple syrup

2 tbsp Greek-style yogurt

⅔ cup blueberries, plus a few whole berries, to decorate

1 tbsp water

1 oz/25 g white chocolate, grated, to decorate

MAKES 6

Gingerbread People

★ Preheat the oven to 375°F/190°C. Sift the flour, ginger, and baking soda into a large mixing bowl. Add the butter and rub into the flour with your fingertips until it resembles fine breadcrumbs. Mix in the sugar.

★ Warm the syrup in a small saucepan until runny, then add to the flour mixture with the beaten egg. Mix to form a soft dough, then knead lightly until smooth. If the dough is too sticky, add a little extra flour.

★ Roll out the dough on a lightly floured work surface then, using a cutter, make the gingerbread people. Place on a lightly greased baking sheet and cook for 10 minutes, or until just crisp and golden. Let cool.

★ Use the chocolate candies to make eyes and buttons, and attach the orange jelly and the lemon cake decorations to make mouths, securing with a little strawberry jam.

1¼ cups all-purpose flour

2 tsp ground ginger

½ tsp baking soda

4 tbsp butter or margarine

scant ½ cup brown sugar

2 tbsp dark corn syrup

1 egg, beaten

TO DECORATE

sugar-coated chocolate candies and orange jelly and lemon cake decorations

1 tbsp strawberry jam

MAKES 6

Mini Strawberry Cheesecakes

★ Line 6 holes of a muffin pan with muffin paper liners.

★ Melt the butter in a small pan over low heat, then let cool. Put the oats in a food processor and blend briefly to break them up, then put into a bowl, add the nuts and melted butter, and mix well. Divide the mixture between the paper liners and press down well. Let chill for 30 minutes.

★ Preheat the oven to 300°F/150°C. Beat the ricotta cheese with the sugar and lemon rind and juice in a bowl. Add the egg, egg yolk, and cottage cheese and mix well. Spoon into the muffin liners and bake in the preheated oven for 30 minutes. Turn off the oven, but let the cheesecakes stand in the oven until completely cold.

★ Peel the kiwi and dice the flesh, and slice the strawberries. Remove the paper liners, top each cheesecake with the fruit, and serve.

generous 5½ tbsp unsalted butter

scant 1 cup rolled oats

heaping 2 tbsp chopped hazelnuts

1 cup ricotta cheese

¼ cup packed brown sugar

finely grated rind of 1 lemon, and juice of ½ lemon

1 egg, plus 1 egg yolk

scant ¾ cup cottage cheese

1 kiwi

6 large strawberries

MAKES 6

INDEX